KOI CARP CULTIVATION

A Step-By-Step Approach To Successful Koi Farming

Transform Your Passion For Koi Into A Profitable Venture With Expert Tips On Breeding And Care

Dr. Fabian Felicity

Table of Contents

Introduction

Koi carp have fascinated enthusiasts and amateurs for ages, with their vivid colors, elegant motions, and cultural importance. These Japanese ornamental fish are recognized not only for their beautiful look but also for the delicate skill of Koi carp rearing.

In this inquiry, we look at the fundamentals of Koi carp farming, from choosing the proper kinds to constructing an optimum breeding habitat.

CHAPTER ONE

The Fascinating World Of Koi Carp

Koi carp, also known as Cyprinus carpio, is a kind of common carp that has been intentionally developed for its unique colors and patterns. Koi originated in Japan in the seventeenth century and swiftly became a symbol of good fortune, wealth, and tenacity.

Their popularity grew worldwide, and they are now appreciated by pond caretakers, painters, and enthusiasts alike.

Koi carp are distinguished by their diverse color and pattern palette, which includes brilliant shades of red, orange, yellow, green, blue, indigo, and violet. These hues look well with dramatic patterns like Kohaku (white with red markings), Taisho Sanshoku or Sanke (white with red and black markings), and Showa Sanshoku or Showa (black with red and white markings). The variety of colors and patterns gives Koi a distinct appeal, transforming them from fish into living art.

Essentials Of Koi Carp Cultivation

Cultivating Koi carp requires a detailed awareness of their fundamental requirements, developmental phases, and general health. Whether you are a seasoned breeder or a newbie, there are some important aspects to consider for effective Koi carp production.

First and foremost, Koi needs a proper environment. A well-designed pond with proper filtration, aeration, and enough room is required. Koi carp thrive in areas with consistent water conditions, therefore frequent testing and care are required. Proper water quality promotes fish health and vigor, resulting in optimum growth and color development.

Feeding is an important part of Koi carp culture. A well-balanced and nutritious food is critical for the fish's overall health. High-quality Koi food contains critical nutrients, improves coloring, and strengthens immune systems. Feeding regimens should be constant, and portion amounts should be tailored to the fish's size and growth stage.

Additionally, knowing the life cycles of Koi is critical for effective breeding. From fry (young Koi) to fingerlings and finally mature adults, each stage needs special care and attention. Monitoring growth rates, providing correct nutrition, and dividing various age groups are all important techniques in Koi carp production.

Choosing The Right Koi Varieties For Your Farm

Choosing the right Koi varieties is an important part of successful cultivation because it affects the overall aesthetic appeal of your pond. With so many colors and patterns to choose from, selecting Koi that complement one another results in a visually stunning and harmonious display.

Some popular Koi varieties include the Kohaku, with its simple yet striking white and red pattern, the Showa, with its black, red, and white markings, and the elegant Ogon, with a single metallic color. Each variety has its distinct charm, and breeders frequently form personal preferences based on their desired pond aesthetics.

When choosing Koi, evaluate body conformation, fin quality, and general health. Look for fish that have a well-balanced physique, symmetrical patterning, and bright colors. High-quality Koi often have robust and elegant movements that demonstrate their vigor and health.

Creating The Ideal Environment For Koi Breeding

Successful Koi breeding requires meticulous planning and consideration of environmental factors. Water temperature, spawning structures, and breeding partner selection are all important aspects for creating the optimum breeding habitat.

Koi normally reproduce in the spring, when water temperatures increase. To stimulate spawning, gradually raise the temperature of the breeding pond's water. Providing appropriate spawning structures, such as plants or special mats, allows the Koi to lay their eggs and encourages effective fertilization.

Selecting breeding couples is a vital step in the reproduction process. To produce the desired offspring, choose healthy, adult Koi with similar colors and patterns. The breeding process must be strictly monitored, since Koi parents may devour their eggs or fry if not adequately overseen.

In conclusion, the world of Koi carp is a mesmerizing combination of art, science, and cultural importance. Understanding the fundamentals of Koi carp growth, from constructing the optimum habitat to choosing the proper types, enables lovers to appreciate the beauty of these ornamental fish while contributing to their well-being and proliferation. As custodians of living art, people who step into the universe of Koi carp find themselves involved in a wonderful and ever-fascinating voyage.

CHAPTER TWO

Nutritional Requirements Of Koi: Feeding Strategies For Optimal Growth

Koi, decorative variations of common carp, are prized for their vivid colors and elegant swimming styles. Understanding koi's dietary requirements is critical for maintaining their aesthetic traits and general well-being.

Feeding strategies are critical in achieving optimal growth and maintaining the vitality of these prized fish.

Koi are omnivorous, which means they eat both plant and animal matter. A well-balanced diet is necessary to promote their growth, coloration, and immune system. High-quality koi pellets are a staple in their diet, providing important nutrients like proteins, fats, vitamins, and minerals. It is critical to select a well-formulated pellet that caters to the specific needs of koi, ensuring they receive the proper balance of nutrients for their overall health.

Feeding frequency is another important aspect of koi nutrition. Overfeeding can cause water quality problems and obesity, reducing the fish's well-being.

Underfeeding, on the other hand, can lead to stunted growth and compromised immune function.

Establishing a consistent feeding schedule, ideally two to three times per day ensures that koi receive adequate nutrition while not overburdening the pond ecosystem.

Water Quality Management For Koi Ponds

The health of Koi is inextricably linked to the quality of water in their ponds. Proper water quality management is essential for a healthy koi population. Monitoring and controlling parameters like pH, ammonia, nitrite, nitrate, and dissolved oxygen levels is critical.

Maintaining an ideal pH level is critical for the health of koi. pH fluctuations can cause stress in fish and compromise their immune systems. Regular testing and adjustments are necessary to ensure the pond water remains within the ideal pH range for koi, typically between 7.0 and 8.5.

Ammonia and nitrite are harmful byproducts of fish waste and uneaten food. Effective filtration systems, along with frequent water changes, can minimize these dangerous compounds. Nitrate, a less harmful byproduct, should also be maintained at acceptable levels by water changes and the use of adequate biological filtering.

Dissolved oxygen is necessary for the respiratory activity of koi. Aeration devices, such as air stones or waterfalls, improve oxygen exchange at the pond's surface. Adequate dissolved oxygen levels are particularly critical during warmer months when oxygen solubility diminishes.

Health And Disease Management In Koi Carp

Maintaining the health of koi needs a proactive approach to illness prevention and a prompt reaction to possible health concerns. Regular monitoring of fish behavior, appetite, and physical condition is crucial to early discovery.

Quarantine precautions are required for new additions to the pond, to avoid the entrance of infections. Monitoring water quality, preventing overcrowding, and establishing a healthy dietary plan contribute greatly to illness prevention.

Additionally, regular health exams by a skilled veterinarian may help detect and manage possible abnormalities before they progress.

Common diseases affecting koi include parasites, bacterial infections, and viral disorders. Prompt and precise diagnosis is critical for successful therapy. Medicated meals, quarantine protocols, and tailored therapies might be applied depending on the individual condition. Regular pond management, including cleaning and disinfection, minimizes the likelihood of disease outbreaks.

Breeding Methods: From Spawning To Fry Care

Breeding koi may be a pleasant but complex task that demands meticulous preparation and supervision. Understanding the reproductive habits of koi is critical for effective breeding. In a controlled setting, spawning is triggered by adjusting water temperature, adding spawning mats, and creating an atmosphere suitable for courting.

Once spawning has occurred, collecting and fertilizing the eggs is a difficult task. The fertilized eggs are subsequently transported to a separate breeding tank or incubator, where they develop into fry. Proper nutrition is essential for the growing fry, and specialist fry chow is often utilized to suit their specific nutritional needs.

As the fry develops, the environment must be checked and modified properly. Gradual acclimation to a bigger pond prepares them to join the main koi population. Successful breeding requires experience and a dedication to providing ideal circumstances throughout the whole process, from spawning to fry care.

CHAPTER THREE

Growth And Development Stages Of Koi

Koi grows and develops in several phases, each with its own set of traits and concerns. Understanding these phases is critical for effective treatment and management.

The first stage, the fry stage, starts with hatching and continues until the fish reach a size of around one inch. During this phase, they are fragile and need specialist care to guarantee sufficient nourishment and predator protection.

During the fingerling stage, the koi grows from one to four inches. This stage is critical for the creation of color patterns, and sufficient nourishment remains a key. Monitoring water quality and giving a well-balanced diet helps to promote healthy development.

Koi begin to exhibit more distinct colors when they reach the juvenile stage, which ranges from four to twelve inches in length. Because developing fish are more vulnerable to environmental stresses, feeding, and pond management must be prioritized at this period.

Finally, throughout the sub-adult and adult phases, color development continues and full size is achieved. During these periods, maintaining ideal water quality, eating a balanced diet, and taking illness preventive measures are critical to the koi's lifespan and vitality.

In conclusion, obtaining optimum koi growth and well-being requires a thorough grasp of their dietary requirements, water quality management, health and disease issues, breeding procedures, and growth and development phases.

Implementing efficient tactics in each of these areas helps to ensure the overall success of preserving and enjoying these gorgeous fish in a pond environment.

Marketing Strategies For Your Koi Farm

Koi farming, or the cultivation of these bright and treasured ornamental fish, has grown in popularity across the globe. As a koi farmer, you must not only concentrate on breeding and caring for your fish but also on successful marketing methods to ensure your company's success. Here are some effective marketing methods for your koi farm.

1. Identify your target market.

Understanding your target market is essential for building successful marketing tactics. Determine if prospective buyers are interested in koi as decorative fish for ponds and gardens. This might include enthusiasts, landscapers, and even corporations who build ponds and landscaping. Customize your marketing efforts to meet the unique demands and tastes of your target audience.

2. Create an online presence.

In the digital era, a good online presence is critical for every organization. Create a professional website that showcases your koi farm, highlights the many kinds you sell, and provides useful information on koi maintenance. Use social media to communicate with prospective consumers and publish compelling information, such as videos of your koi, instructive postings about koi care, and customer reviews.

3.   Utilize   Search   Engine Optimization (SEO).

It is vital to optimize your website for search engines so that prospective clients may discover your koi farm online. Conduct keyword research for koi farming and include these keywords organically in your website's content. This will increase the visibility of your website on search engines, making it more likely that interested parties will find your koi farm while looking for information or supplies.

4. Establish partnerships and collaborations.

Form ties with local garden shops, pet stores, and pond-building companies. Collaborate on collaborative campaigns or events to raise knowledge about your koi farm in the local community. Offering discounts or special packages to clients suggested by these partners is an efficient approach to encourage cooperation.

5. Attend trade shows and expositions.

Participating in relevant aquaculture and pet trade events and expos may help your koi farm reach a larger audience. Set up a very appealing booth to display your koi, provide informational pamphlets, and interact with possible consumers. These events are a great way to network with other companies, learn about industry trends, and attract new customers.

CHAPTER FOUR
Legal And Regulatory Considerations For Koi Carp Cultivation

While creating marketing tactics is critical to the profitability of your koi farm, you must also negotiate the legal and regulatory environment of koi carp production. Understanding and sticking to these issues guarantees that your firm works ethically and legally.

1. Obtain the necessary permits and licenses.

Before you begin your koi farm, investigate and secure the necessary permissions and licenses. These may differ based on your region, so consult with local authorities and regulatory agencies. Compliance with rules guarantees that your koi farm works lawfully, avoiding possible legal ramifications from non-compliance.

2. Biosecurity Measures

Implementing biosecurity measures is critical for preventing disease transmission within your koi population and associated environmental consequences. Develop and adhere to methods for controlling and monitoring your fish's health, as well as quarantine measures for new arrivals. This not only protects your koi but also indicates a dedication to safe and ethical farming.

3.   Environmental Impact Assessment

Conduct an environmental impact study to determine the possible implications of your koi farm on the local ecology. This might involve evaluating water use, waste management, and the possible effect on local fauna. Adhering to environmental rules not only assures your koi farm's viability but also helps to maintain a favorable public image.

4. Complying with Animal Welfare Standards

Maintaining good standards of animal welfare is both a moral commitment and a legal mandate. Familiarize yourself with and follow the animal welfare requirements for koi farming. This involves giving enough room, good water quality, and suitable nourishment for your koi. Regular veterinarian inspections and a timely reaction to any symptoms of sickness are critical components of safeguarding your fish's health.

Troubleshooting Common Issues With Koi Farming

While koi farming may be gratifying, it is not without obstacles. Addressing and fixing common difficulties as soon as possible is critical to keeping your koi farm healthy and growing.

1. Water Quality Management

Maintaining proper water quality is critical to the health of your koi. Regularly test and monitor pH, ammonia, and oxygen levels. If problems emerge, take early remedial action, which may include modifying water parameters, improving aeration, or applying water treatments. Poor water quality may cause stress and sickness in koi, reducing their general well-being.

2. Disease Prevention & Control

Koi are vulnerable to a variety of illnesses, and early detection and treatment are crucial for averting major epidemics. Set up a thorough quarantine policy for new arrivals, do frequent health checks, and isolate any ill fish. Collaborate with a trained aquatic veterinarian to develop disease preventive and treatment protocols.

3. Proper Nutrition

Ensuring that your koi have a balanced and healthy food is critical for their development and general health. Monitor eating patterns and tailor the food to your koi's age and size. Overfeeding or offering an uneven diet may cause health problems as well as influence the pond's water quality. Consult with aquaculture nutrition specialists to create a feeding plan that is suited to your koi's requirements.

4. Pond Maintenance

Regular care of your koi ponds is essential to avoid problems like algae development, blocked filters, and debris collection. Perform periodic equipment inspections, clean filters as required, and remove trash from the pond. Neglecting pond upkeep might result in low water quality and an unpleasant environment for your koi.

Conclusion

Operating a successful koi farm requires a multidimensional strategy that includes efficient marketing techniques, adherence to legal and regulatory concerns, and timely debugging of frequent problems.

You may provide a solid marketing foundation for your koi farm by defining your target market, developing a strong internet presence, and forming strategic relationships.

Simultaneously, navigating the legal environment, establishing biosecurity controls, and maintaining compliance with animal welfare requirements are critical to your company's ethical and legal operations. Finally, diagnosing typical concerns with water quality, illness prevention, feeding, and pond upkeep is critical for running a healthy and flourishing koi farm.

By incorporating these factors into your koi farming operation, you may improve its sustainability, profitability, and reputation in the aquaculture sector.